BRIGHT
IDEA
BOOKS

HORSE RIDING Instructor

by Lisa Harkrader

CAPSTONE PRESS
a capstone imprint

Bright Idea Books are published by Capstone Press
1710 Roe Crest Drive, North Mankato, Minnesota 56003
www.mycapstone.com

Library of Congress Cataloging-in-Publication Data
Names: Harkrader, Lisa, author.
Title: Horse riding instructor / by Lisa Harkrader.
Description: North Mankato, Minnesota : Bright Idea Books, an imprint of
   Capstone Press, [2019] | Series: Jobs with animals | Audience: Age 9-12. |
   Audience: Grade 4 to 6. | Includes bibliographical references and index.
Identifiers: LCCN 2018035986 | ISBN 9781543557886 (hardcover : alk. paper) |
   ISBN 9781543558203 (ebook) | ISBN 9781543560503 (paperback)
Subjects: LCSH: Horsemanship--Vocational guidance--Juvenile literature.
Classification: LCC SF309.2 .H37 2019 | DDC 798.2--dc23
LC record available at https://lccn.loc.gov/2018035986

Editorial Credits
Editor: Meg Gaertner
Designer: Becky Daum
Production Specialist: Dan Peluso

Photo Credits
iStockphoto: alacatr, 21, Arostynov, 20, asiseeit, 5, CasarsaGuru, 10, Drazen_, 10–11,
EMPPhotography, 23, fotokostic, 16–17, Image Source, 22, vgajic, 19, Wavebreakmedia, cover;
Shutterstock Images: gorillaimages, 25, Mikhail Pogosov, 12–13, My Good Images, 6, 28,
nazarovsergey, 30–31, sanyanwuji, 26–27, Skumer, 15, Tanja Esser, 9, Vagengeim, 14

TABLE OF CONTENTS

CHAPTER 1

RIDING
Instructor

A woman leads a horse into a large ring.

She shows a boy how to get on the horse.

The boy sits in the **saddle**.

The woman shows him how to stay steady. She shows him how to hold the **reins**. The woman is a horse riding instructor.

The instructor uses a lunge line. The student can focus on sitting properly instead of steering the horse.

Instructors might own their own horses or work with a school's horses.

RIDER AND TEACHER

Riding instructors are experts at riding horses. They are also a kind of coach. They teach people how to ride horses. Do you like to ride horses? Do you enjoy teaching other people? Maybe a job as a horse riding instructor is for you.

HORSES

There are more than 350 types of horses.

CHAPTER 2

THE
Work

Riding instructors work with horses. Instructors care for horses. They **groom** horses. They brush horses' coats. They clean horses' hooves. They ride often.

Instructors know how to **tack up** a horse. They can put a saddle on a horse's back. They can put a **bridle** on a horse's head. Riders use the bridle to guide the horse.

Saddles must be tight around the horse's belly or the rider might fall off.

THE STUDENTS

Riding instructors teach people about horses. They teach people of all ages. They teach beginners. They teach those who have been riding a long time. They teach people with disabilities.

An instructor teaches a student to balance in the saddle.

Younger students might ride ponies instead of horses. Ponies are smaller than horses.

Instructors know how to give helpful feedback. Sometimes they teach classes with large groups of students. Sometimes they give private lessons. They teach one student at a time.

THE LESSONS

Riding instructors teach many things. They teach students to groom horses. They teach students how to tack up horses. They teach students to ride at different **gaits**. A gait is the speed and way a horse moves. Horses have four main gaits. A walk is the slowest gait. A gallop is the fastest. The trot and canter come in between.

FEEL THE BEAT

Each gait has a certain rhythm. It has a certain number of beats. A trot is a two-beat gait. A canter is a three-beat gait.

A person who rides horses in races is called a jockey.

13

In dressage, horses learn to step in a particular controlled way.

TEACHING SKILLS

Some riding instructors teach specific moves. They teach students to jump. They teach **dressage**. A horse makes skilled moves in dressage. The rider guides the horse through the moves.

In show jumping, students and horses jump over obstacles.

Riding instructors are patient. They stay calm. This helps students learn. It also helps horses behave.

Instructors are in charge of safety. They help make sure the horses and students stay safe. Horses are strong. They can kick. Riders can fall from their backs.

A calm instructor keeps riders calm as they learn different skills.

CHAPTER 3

THE
Workplace

Riding instructors work in many places. They spend a lot of time in horse barns. They spend time in riding rings. Some rings are outdoors. Others are inside big buildings.

Riding instructors may clean horses' stalls when they aren't teaching.

Western saddles are big and heavy. They spread the weight of the rider over more of the horse.

SCHOOLS

Some riding instructors work at riding schools. Many instructors may work at the same school. The instructors teach lessons to students. Many of their students take lessons for years. Some take part in horse shows. Instructors often go to the shows. They coach their students at the shows.

RIDING STYLES

Two main styles of riding are Western and English. The styles use different saddles.

English saddles are small and light. They give the rider closer contact with the horse's back.

Helmets help keep riders safe.

CAMPS AND RANCHES

Some riding instructors work at summer camps. They teach small groups of campers. Many of the campers are beginners. Other instructors work at guest ranches. A guest ranch is a vacation spot. People stay at the ranch for a short time. Instructors teach ranch guests basic riding skills. They lead people on trail rides.

Ranch guests may go on trail rides.

CHAPTER 4

GETTING THE
Job

Most riding instructors do not need to go to college. But they must be expert riders. Some instructors get special training. They earn a **certificate**. The certificate shows they know how to teach riding.

Riding instructors teach students to ride safely in different surroundings.

A love of horses is necessary for this job.

ON THE JOB

Riding instructors make $30,000 to $40,000 per year. Most work year-round. Some teach on weekends. At camps and ranches they may work only in the summer.

Instructors teach riders to ride and care for horses. They get to meet new people. They can share their love of horses with others.

GLOSSARY

bridle
straps that fit over a horse's head

certificate
an official document that people can earn by demonstrating a specific skill

dressage
the art of training a horse to make special movements

gait
the manner and speed with which a horse moves

groom
to care for an animal by brushing and cleaning it

reins
long straps attached to either side of a horse's bridle that are used to guide the horse

saddle
a seat strapped to a horse's back

tack up
to put riding gear, such as a saddle and bridle, on a horse

OTHER JOBS TO CONSIDER

FARRIER

Farriers trim horses' hooves. They may put horseshoes on horses' hooves. This helps protect the hooves.

GROOM

Grooms take care of horses. They work in a horse barn or stable. They feed and groom the horses.

HORSE TRAINER

Horse trainers train horses for racing, showing, or other events. They teach horses to behave. They train horses to move in certain ways.

JOCKEY

Jockeys ride horses during horse races. They are expert riders. They have to meet certain weight requirements.

ACTIVITY

TACK UP!

Horse riding instructors are expert riders. But they have to tack up a horse before they can ride. Tack is the riding gear put on horses. Tack includes:

- saddles
- saddle pads
- stirrups
- bridles
- reins
- bits

Look online for information about the different gear. Then make a poster about what you learned. You can draw pictures. You can cut pictures out of magazines. Show a horse on your poster. Show the horse's tack. Label each kind of tack. Write what it is used for. Share your poster with family and friends.

FURTHER RESOURCES

Want to learn about riding horses?
Check out these resources:

Bratton, Donna Bowman. *Saddle Up! Riding and Competitions for Horse Lovers.* North Mankato, Minn.: Capstone Press, 2015.

DK Find Out! Horseback Riding
www.dkfindout.com/us/sports/horseback-riding/

Eschbach, Andrea. *Kids Riding with Confidence: Fun, Beginner Lessons to Build Trusting, Safe Partnerships with Horses.* North Pomfret, Vt.: Trafalgar Square, 2014.

Curious about horses in general? Learn more here:

DK Find Out! What Is a Horse?
www.dkfindout.com/us/animals-and-nature/horses/what-is-horse/

Jazynka, Kitson. *Gallop! 100 Fun Facts about Horses.* Washington, D.C.: National Geographic, 2018.

INDEX